SECOND INCOME

A guide To Making Money From Home

J.A. FLORENTINO

Second Income: A guide To Making Money from Home

Introduction

With job postings still rare, job security dispersing, and wages seemingly stagnant at best case scenario, numerous individuals are attempting to set up various surges of  income. This has become a keen technique in the event that you experience difficulty leaving your home or primary position to land a secondary job.

Maybe you are raising children and you are focused on not using childcare. Or possibly you are a bit older and cannot commit to a full-time job. You may be harmed or disabled, making it troublesome for you to leave your home every day. Whatever your reason is, in case you are stuck at home the greater part of the day, you have most likely wondered about the salary you could be earning by engaging a work-from-home job or maintaining your own business.

J.A. Florentino

Good news: There are a lot of genuine approaches to gain additional cash sitting right where you are at this moment. Some of them include beginning your own particular small business, while others mean working for another person utilizing your home as an office.

These tries are not without traps and difficulties, however, so before we take a gander at some genuine approaches to profit from your home, how about we audit a couple of things that you ought to maintain a strategic distance from. Lamentably, on the off chance that you need to acquire a legit living from home, you are a typical focus of tricksters, particularly in these economically tough times. Be that as it may, if you remember these basic guidelines, you won't turn into a casualty of one of the numerous home scams.

Table of Contents

HOW TO MAKE MONEY BLOGGING

Here are the five essential steps that you need to follow to profit from blogging. I will explain them in more detail as we go, with a detailed guide on #5.

1. Establish your home base

2. Produce valuable content

3. Build connections

4. Grow your platform (and branch out)

5. Choose and execute streams of income

If you discover yourself getting overwhelmed and excited as you read through, you are ordinary! Try not to stress; I will give you a few tips for beginning at the end of the guide.

Okay, how about we start it.

1. Set up your home base

If you want to profit from blogging, clearly, you will require a blog. This is the simple part (regardless of the possibility that you are not technically-inclined).

2. Produce important substance

Once you have an online journal, write. Draw from your ability and encounter and compose informative posts and articles about the chosen subject. Make your content valuable and worthwhile. Keeping in mind the end goal to profit, you must have visitors. However, with a specific end

goal to have visitors, you must have content worthy for them to visit.

Composing and producing content is the tedious part. It will be a while before you begin receiving income. There is no other way to get around this. There are no alternate routes. We all need to invest our energy to achieve something.

3. Construct connections

While you make your content, begin building real and genuine connections by means of social media, online networking, commenting on different blog sites, forums and so forth. Connect with individuals in your niche. Discover individuals who could utilize the information you give. Become more acquainted with them, interact, be friendly and offer no-strings-attached tidbits of your expertise. Building authentic relationships is vital for various reasons:

- You will build up a reputation of being dependable, trustworthy and generous.

- Your site will be found. Individuals won't normally discover your site in the event that you do not put yourself out there.

- It is exceptionally conceivable these relationships will transform into significantly more than only associates to talk with on the web. These individuals will probably support you later on, and more than that, they may get to be fabulous, deep-rooted, life-long companions.

4. Develop your platform (and branch out)

Continue developing in the learning of your art so the substance you deliver gets extraordinary. Utilize your blog to get exposure, build authority, gain their trust, and be useful.

5. Choose and implement streams of income

This is the part you have been sitting tight for—the genuine ways individuals profit from blogging.

There are various ways bloggers profit. Every blogger has an alternate blend of income streams. There is no "right" way. What's more, that is the excellence of it. There are unlimited potential outcomes. You need to discover a mix that works for you.

The following is a rundown of pay streams bloggers receive, separated into five fundamental classifications:

- Advertising
- Affiliate Marketing
- Digital Products
- Physical Products
- Services

Advertising

Dissimilar to most of the other categories, promoting or advertising is about producing salary, specifically from your blog, site or other digital asset(s).

Display Ads

Display ads are graphics or images, like promotions in a magazine. Normally, they are situated on your site in the sidebar, header, footer or inside of your content. Once in a while, they are alluded to as banner advertisements.

Some ad networks, as Google Adsense, are moderately simple to get into and are anything but difficult to set up. Other advertisement systems, however, are specific in who they acknowledge. Some advertisement systems are: Google Adsense, Blogads, BlogHer, Beacon Ads, Federated Media, Sovrn, (earlier Lijit), Media.net, Rivit and Sway. There are many more. Once you get included in your special niche's group of bloggers you will find out about others.

Affiliate marketing

As an affiliate marketing, you advance another person's item or service in a post or somewhere else. You link to that item or service utilizing your unique affiliate link.

When somebody clicks on that link and makes a buy (or finishes a craved action set by the organization) you gain a commission.

Digital Products

Audio/Video

You can offer music or video that others can use as intros or outros, such as Audio Jungle or iStockPhoto.

Applications, Plugins or Themes

If you have a skill for code-writing and can compose your own themes or plugins, you can offer them at a spot like Creative Market. Some plugin creators offer their plugins for nothing, yet request donations.

Domains

Do you have a domain collecting issue? Did you know you could sell them for a profit? Attempt at a site like Sedo.

Ecourses/Webinars/Online Workshops

You could do a wide range of things with this sort of digital product. You would not need to go huge the first run through around. Try things out by holding a local presentation first. Develop greater as you take in the ropes and make sense of what works and what does not.

Photographs

Are you a photographer? Illustrator? Why not offer your photographs on a site like iStockphoto or Foap?

Selling Blogs & Websites

Numerous bloggers have sold their blogs or sites for 4-, 5-, 6-and even 7-figure sums.

Physical Products

Books

For some bloggers, their blogs have assisted them with selling books, both self and traditionally published. I have heard over and over again that traditional publishers will not commonly consider your composition in the event that you do not have a blog first.

Conferences, Classes or Special Events

Consider facilitating a social gathering, and presenting a "physical" product, since it includes a trade of something substantial (for this situation, cash for a ticket to an experience). You can also do greater events, like long seminars or workshops, or even multi-day gatherings.

Handmade Products

Are you crafty? Try selling on Etsy or Handmade at Amazon.

You can set up your own particular shop for nothing and it is easy to begin. It is not all that easy to emerge from the crowd, so that will probably be your greatest test.

Services

Think about this like freelancing. On the
off chance that you have an ability (and
who doesn't?), why not offer your
service(s) by means of the web? It does
not need to be PC related. Consider ways you can utilize your already

picked up abilities to support you and put them on the web. This will

be discussed in the next chapter.

Freelancer's Guide to Making Money

I would say that one of the most ideal approaches to profit is to begin freelancing. I am going to say without a moment's hesitation that anybody can freelance. Yes, anybody! In the spirit of profiting, I needed to share my rendition of a freelancer's guide for profiting. In this chapter, I am going to cover what you have to do to begin freelancing and how to be successful in it.

Recognize Your Skill Set

The most critical piece of freelancing is understanding what you can sell. Most freelancers sell their services. Those can be composing content, giving organization ideas, product design, online marketing, blog management, website design, website testing, coding, and many more. There  is an extensive variety of services that individuals can do. They may be hard to discover, yet, they are still there.

Everybody has some sort of marketable expertise. Whether it be sufficient for a full-time occupation or not is another story. Individuals have a tendency to be great at many things. Many do not consider selling that expertise to others. This is normally on the grounds that a few individuals simply do not think outside the box. If you want to succeed at being a freelancer, then, you have to comprehend your skill and check whether it is marketable.

What's Your Value Proposition

Hold up? My value what? Before I begin

diving into the VP, as I like to call it, I

am going to toss down a little definition

for you. This is the means by which

Investopedia characterizes a value

proposition: a business or marketing

statement that summarizes why a

consumer should buy a product or use a service. This statement

should convince a potential consumer that one particular product or

service will add more value or better solve a problem than other

similar offerings.

In the freelancing world, you are most likely not going to be separated

from everyone else in the services you offer. I can just about be sure

of that. In the event that you have a one of a kind service, then you

may need to think about making a full time business out of it. That is

just in case you have an awesome value proposition. This

announcement is to characterize why your service ought to be picked

above all others. Why might your service be any better? What makes

your service uncommon? These are a couple of things that you have to answer when you think of your value proposition. Do you charge less, yet deliver more? Do you simply kick ass and you ought to be paid for it? Before you turn into a freelancer, you have to comprehend your value proposition.

By what means Will You Market Your Services?

Okay, you have now made sense of your expertise and what separates you from the pack. Congrats! Here comes the hardest part in a freelancer's job. You need to market yourself with a specific end goal to get customers. Anybody that has freelanced before realizes that advertising can be a hard thing to do. You need to speak to individuals searching for your abilities in an ocean of consultants. This is particularly genuine on the web. You better know how to market yourself. There are a couple of ways that can separate you from others.

Begin a blog – Running a blog can be an incredible approach to meet individuals in the specialty you are focusing on. Clearly, you will need to cover subjects that identify with your abilities. You can find jobs by networking with different bloggers.

Be Active on Social Media – Connect and network with other individuals. When you are dynamic on social media and speak with those in your specialty, you can make companions. Networking is key and social media empowers that network that much more.

Join a Freelance Jobs Board – There are an excess of jobs sheets out there to name. In the matter of freelancing, Odesk, Elance and Fiverr are extraordinary alternatives. You can, without much of a stretch, set up an account and begin selling your services. Try not to be disheartened if you do not land a position immediately. There are numerous different consultants on these sheets to contend with, however, simply stay with your value proposition.

Contact Companies Directly – This system may not generally be effective, but you can and will land positions from it if you are great. If you know of an organization that could utilize your services, then connect with them. Get in touch with them and check whether they need assistance. You never know where it will lead.

Pricing and Delivery

Welcome to the next stride in pricing. If you are going to sell services, then you better realize what you need to charge. This is a hard thing to accomplish for most freelancers. The reason is that the information to set right rates and delivery times originates from experience. You do not get experience until you have a couple of finished jobs under your belt. This is the place you should be adaptable. Your initial few jobs may pay you less, however, they will get you experience. If you hop into discussions about estimating with a high value, then it will be a quick kill. This is particularly genuine if you have no certifications to back up your pricing or any testimonials. Pricing is genuinely a workmanship when you freelance, therefore, you should not be hesitant to switch it up.

When you begin working and selling your aptitudes, you should deliver. This stride originates from experience. In the event that you are writing, you have to know to what extent and how long it will take. If the people that employed you inquire as to whether you can complete said errand in a specific amount of time, you better know whether you can complete it. There is an excess of different specialists out there that will accept your job in an instant. Try not to miss your due dates. If you think you are going to miss your due date, connect with your contact and let them know why. Be straightforward. That will keep you at work.

So, there you go. These are my keys to profiting as a freelancer. You have to know your expertise set, comprehend your value proposition, market based value proposition, then value it right, and deliver. This aide may make it sound simple, yet, there are not many freelancers that profit. Simply do not get disheartened. This is not a get rich brisk sort of thing. You will not turn into a tycoon overnight. You might never get to be one. The purpose of freelancing is to win additional cash as an afterthought and do something that you appreciate. It may even transform into a full time job, like our companions at Club Thrifty and Making Sense of Cents.

Being a freelancer has a great deal of advantages – you can work from anyplace you like, you make up your own particular standards, you do not need to worry about trifling office governmental issues, there is less push included, and you get the opportunity to invest a ton more energy with your loved ones. In any case, not having a steady job implies that you will be carrying on with a wanderer's life. Sort of like an online ronin, a masterless samurai meandering the virtual wastes. All things considered, there are sites you can access to search for incredible freelance open doors, so, do not lose hope. Here are twenty awesome freelance sites you should look at.

1. Elance

Elance is one of the best sites to search for freelance work of different kinds. Programmers, designers, writers, IT professionals, translators, attorneys, financial advisers, everybody is welcome and there is a lot of work to go around. You can set up a profile fairly quickly and charge an hourly rate, or have a set cost for every individual project. You get evaluated depending on how well you do.

2. Freelancer

It has been around since 2004 and it has a substantial after. It is a spot where services are outsourced to freelancers in various fields, including: web design, writing, promoting, and data entry, in addition to other things.

3. Guru

Guru.com is a genuinely large network that interfaces organizations and freelancers. As expressed on the site, they are interested in work on "technical, creative, or business projects". Therefore, there are a lot of opportunities for a wide range of freelancers from software engineers and game developers to interpreters, engineers, and lawyers.

4. iFreelance

iFreelance is a wide freelance network with classifications that incorporate photography, videography, advertising, traditional art, writing, interpretation, architecture, building, graphic design, accounting, and administrative support. It is easy to set up an account and begin searching for a task you can add to.

5. PeoplePerHour

Make an engaging profile, search for jobs, send propositions, and make a short video advancing your services. It is all exceptionally clear with PeoplePerHour.com – you discover a customer, give a quality service, and get reviewed.

6. Tuts Plus Jobs

This is an awesome job board for programmers, designers and developers, as well as copywriters, and editors. It has an easy to use interface and permits you to rapidly discover and apply for jobs most appropriate to your specific expertise set.

7. ProBlogger

An amazing job board for skilled writers, ProBlogger makes discovering the right written work opportunities unimaginably basic. Simply click on the work postings you need and take after the directions.

8. Freelance Writing Gigs

This is another incredible site for every writer out there. Posting a notice will cost you around $10, however, it will allow you to showcase your writing expertise and give content to those willing to pay for your endeavors. You can, likewise, add to their blog and get some extra exposure by connecting to your blog/site and social media accounts.

9. SmashingJobs

This is a designer's and programmer's paradise, offering a lot of full-time and freelance job opportunities. The site has a perfect and fresh outline which takes into consideration snappy browsing and some proficient job hunting.

10. Odesk

Set up an account and browse 75 diverse job classes and a lot of offers inside of every classification. The thing with oDesk is that there is no invoicing included – your work is followed naturally and you get installments on a week after week premise contingent upon the amount of time you spent on different ventures. Some of the main categories incorporate written work and translation, software development, web development, marketing, and design.

11. Fiverr

Sell your services beginning at $5, that is the slogan and it is very exact. You can offer essentially anything you can consider – write and perform a poem, make DIY projects or promotional videos, and so forth. Some fundamental categories are: writing and translating, online marketing, video and animation, music, programing and graphic design.

12. Freelanced

This is a freelance interpersonal organization where an extensive number of individuals with various types of gifts and aptitudes can meet up, share their portfolios, and search for some online work. There are countless classifications running from inventive scholars, sculptors and music composers to accountants and programmers.

13. Freelance-Writing-Jobs-Online

An assortment of fields to expand on can be found here, extending from arithmetic and material science to science and medication. To sign up you have to round out a structure and sit tight for an affirmation email. After getting the email you may take a competency test and be en route to winning some cash.

14. Pitch Me

A freelancer with some involvement in journalism will feel comfortable on this site. Thoughts are pitched on different themes –

fashion, science, society, and so on – and you can pitch as many thoughts as you like. If somebody loves what you bring to the table, they can then pay you to compose it. It is as straightforward as that.

15. Textbroker

This site furnishes capable writers with an extremely compelling method for getting paid for doing what they excel at. You begin by making a free account and finishing a competency test after which you will be appraised. At that point, if all goes well, you can finish your writer profile and begin searching for composing assignments that suit you.

16. ArtWanted

Artwanted is the ideal spot for artists and photographers to make an online portfolio, get feedback, and sell their fine art on the web. Enlistment is free, yet there is a $5 every month premium membership option that gives you access to some great extra components.

17. 99designs

This is a site where more than 281,579 designers from 192 different nations can associate with potential customers and showcase their work. A customer gives information about his business and a thought of the kind of logo he needs. At that point, the architects send in their work and the customer can select the one he prefers best. You search for design contests, enter the ones you like and do your best to win. As you win more challenges, your status will enhance and you will get more open doors.

18. Simply Hired

This is a major and expansive job chasing site with huge amounts of choices, yet, it is an awesome approach to search for some freelance work, especially if you are an author, graphic designer or web designer. It is anything but difficult to explore and you can rapidly seek through an expansive number of late job offerings in your field.

19. Tutor

As the name recommends, you can turn into an online tutor for families with home-schooled kids, kids in military families, and even schools. There are various subjects and distinctive evaluation levels to browse in the event that you have a more profound comprehension of a subject, for example, math, English or science.

You need to round out an application structure, pass a subject exam and convey a writing sample, perform a mock session to test your showing abilities, and experience a background check before you can begin working.

20. Authentic Jobs

A very much planned and clear job board, AuthenticJobs.com permits you to sift through classifications you are intrigued by and apply for freelance jobs in distinctive fields. The primary center is on web development, web design, application development, project management and UI design.

I trust that you find this information helpful and that you succeed in your freelance vocation. Simply recall to be tolerant and to continue looking. It requires investment to see a few genuine results, however, freelancing can be a satisfying vocation once you get pass the initial stages.

Fun and Easy Money with YouTube Videos

Why Not Use YouTube Earning as a Primary Online Money Option?

It turns into a real dilemma when a person decides to make online earning his main source of income. Most make blogging an essential choice and go for it. Maybe this trend is picked in light of the fact that they are attracted by high CPC values of keywords in

blogging. At that point, why not YouTube? It would be easy to earn money online and, at some point, YouTube would pay you more than what blogging would accomplish for you. What's more, this really remains constant in the first phase of your steps in an online earning world. Along these lines, how about we check the potential and advantages of YouTube monetization over earning from blogs.

1) No domain and hosting cash:

The greatest edge beginning on YouTube is that you are not required to buy any domain or hosting, yet, you can make your online presence by virtue of a channel name. Is it not really cool to get your content hosted by a site which is among the world's top 5 sites and whose servers are available at such a large number of locations in the world? In a nutshell, YouTube will be your home money making strategy with Zero investment needed.

2) It is possible to earn first day on YouTube:

The most wonderful thing with YouTube earning is that you can earn from your video content on first day itself. You can basically make a YouTube account and upload a video (this can be any video which does not disregard YouTube or AdSense terms and conditions). This can be your trek video, or how you made masala dosa in the morning. Individuals have uploaded all kinds of videos and discovered accomplishments from nowhere. At the point when Charlie's dad uploaded that video he would have never thought it would make him millions. Presently, Charlie Bit My Finger is a brand, not only a video. This outcome would be a lifelong dream of an above normal blogger!

3) AdSense Approval via YouTube is easy as well

Most Indian and other South Asian individuals wait for six months, or more, to get their AdSense accounts approved. Yet, if you apply to AdSense through YouTube or Blogger it turns out to be generally easier. You can always add your blog or site to this account once you think you have fulfilled all criteria to get an approved website.

Huge and ready-made platform of audience on YouTube Earning:

When you upload your video, it can be accessible to billions of guests on YouTube and, if your video is catchy and something thrilling, it can surely get you popularity, and you will profit from YouTube videos. Individuals have rocketed their YouTube views in a matter of a day or two and earned a couple of hundred $$$. So, why not pick the camera and shoot something now. Likewise, there are many software available which let you record your screen, therefore, you can do video tutorials effectively by it as well.

How to profit on YouTube?

With your YouTube channel you can earn cash by all sorts of ways. I will quickly share some of the easiest and most well-known approaches to profit.

Google AdSense:

You can adapt your YouTube channel with AdSense. AdSense shows contextual promotions on your YouTube channel and you earn cash when viewers click on the commercial. This is by far the simplest way that different Youtubers are profiting. There are numerous artists who are earning over $2,000 consistently from their YouTube videos.

Sponsored video:

This works awesome when you have an established and popular channel. You can get sponsors for your videos, who might pay you to show their name or quick advertisement at the starting or toward the video's end. A large portion of them use native promoting to showcase their product and it is one extraordinary approach to profit from YouTube.

Affiliate marketing:

This is the thing that lets you earn a huge sum in a short-time. All you need to do is pick the right product, make a video around it, and put the link in the description. You earn per deal, and generally the payout is decent.

YouTube can be a supportive platform for your online earning when you are building your blog; you can even make a profit without using a blog. What's more, once your blog is good to go, you can put the video tutorials of your blog posts on YouTube to earn some extra money. It can even help you by getting guests who are not utilizing Google as a main search engine and your web page is past their reach, till now.

YouTube supports almost all sorts of videos. You can also post videos in a large number of distinctive categories. It can be your trip to Europe or the hotel you stayed at in Spain. You can make tutorials on WordPress, hosting, and other blogging or technical stuff. Additionally, individuals do the reviews of gadgets on YouTube to get benefited from YouTube earning.

Become a Teacher on Udemy & Skillshare

When you consider getting paid to educate about what you know, what rings a bell? Putting up a notice in a local café and hoping for the best? Posting an advertisement on Craigslist?

Fortunately for us, we are no longer constrained to our local area regarding the matter of getting paid to teach our skills. Because of online learning platforms like Udemy and Skillshare, anybody, anyplace, can teach anything.

On the off chance that you think you do not have any skills to educate, reconsider. Most of us are specialists at something, whether it is putting on makeup, baking brownies, or even crafting balloon animals!

J.A. Florentino

Drawing a blank on what you could teach or help others with? Here are some ideas:

- Music lessons

- Photography lessons

- Web programming lessons or services

- Computer repair lessons or services

- Social media consulting

- Cooking or baking lessons

- Fitness instruction

- Nutrition consultations

- Academic tutoring

- Life coaching

- Style consultations

- Beauty consultations

- Gardening help

You get the chance to set the rate for your lessons (most go for between $25-$50). What's more, a few individuals have been truly effective at this – we simply discovered a gentleman who has made $500,000 selling his courses on Udemy.

Earn Money By Helping a Company Name Themselves

Proficient branders are not going anyplace. However, for small organizations that cannot manage the cost of the million dollar price tag, there is another trend called crowdsourcing.  This permits organizations to outsource the creative process to individuals, like you and I, through "naming contests."

There are many naming contests on sites like NamingForce.com and SquadHelp.com. The way it works is that anonymous organizations provide some information about their organization and a prize for the individual who can think of the best name. The prizes are anywhere in the range of $50-$500, with the normal amount at around $100.

For instance, one organization on SquadHelp states that they are an organization that buys used video games and that they will pay $80 to the individual who can propose the best name. Submissions, so far, are "Money 2 Gamers" and "Diversion Epix." Think you can do it better? Try it out here.

Become an Online Tutor

Education is one of the world's leading commercial enterprises and, by the year 2017, the private tutoring market alone is expected to top $100 billion.

Have you ever thought of turning into an online tutor for profit? All things considered, if you have not, you most unquestionably ought to. You can make a few genuine coins by answering student's inquiries, explaining your notes, and uploading tutorials. It is hard to believe, but it is true, that by sharing your insight, you can get paid handsomely.

Try to market your services on a site like AceYourCollegeClasses.com, where top tutors have earned more than $10,000.

Transcription

Transcription is a job that individuals, from time to time, envision themselves doing, yet, inquisitively enough, it is a standout amongst the most stable sources of online jobs accessible at any given time.

The procedure is basic: you listen to an audio file, translate its contents as per the guidelines indicated, turn in the completed product, and get paid.

It, obviously, is very seldom and as easy as that. Considering the unfathomably wide range of topics that your assignments may cover, you may find yourself at a loss when dealing with lingo from particular zones of work, or just disappointed because of segments of a file where the speakers talk over one another and you cannot make out a single word they say.

Transcription is not for everybody, and most online platforms have incredibly high burnout rates. In any case, if you find that you do not mind the work and possess a set of earphones, it may very well be the ticket for you. Further on ahead, you may even need to invest in a pedal – with this, you can knock your speed up even

higher as you will not be able to take your hands off the keyboard in order to speed up, down, or replay parts of a sound document.

Starting rates for transcription work may go as high as $0.6-0.7 for every minute of audio, which is much better than average pay. However, in the event that you are a rookie, it will almost absolutely require you a long time to get past even short audio files. Therefore, your actual amount of earnings will not be high until you get some experience and speed added to your work.

Once you have been doing transcription for some time, you may even find the opportunity to do some media work, which pays extensively better, or you may make it to your customer's shortlist for rush jobs.

At the point when you are searching for transcription jobs, you will notice that they are separated, mostly into four categories, such as:

Medical: this includes translating the notes of medicinal professionals and is viewed as a technical trade, so, any serious workplace will require you to take a training before accepting you into their group. This preparation is mostly quite expensive.

Legal: somewhat more casual than medical transcription, yet at the same time requires a few qualifications, mostly as past involvement in some area related to the law.

General: the catch-all class which amasses all the odd-jobs, for example, conferences, telephone calls, and so forth. This is likely going to be your meat and bones unless you are willing to experience the qualifications to acquire either medical or legal transcription work.

Media: mostly work relating to TV, for example, documentaries or reality TV. They offer a great pay since they are typically deadline-sensitive. As being what is indicated, it is a hard specialty to get into.

Since you have been legitimately cautioned about what you are getting into, we should review some of the best transcription sites to work for.

1. Daily Transcriptions (US-Only)

Daily Transcriptions (DT) gives transcription services running from academic, legitimate and corporate, through multi-lingual. Their pay rate is around $0.7 for every minute for most assignments, and you are ensured work every week.

- Payment methods: Direct deposits.

- Potential earnings: Transcriptionists are paid $0.7, on average, per minute of audio.

- Available amount of work: Indeterminate, assignments are sent specifically to you by means of email.

- Joining requirements: Being a US resident and passing a test, which includes deciphering a genuine audio clip. The test itself is quite troublesome.

- Link: http://www.dailytranscription.com/

2. Focus Forward (US-Only)

Focus Forward (FF) is another site that is continually searching for new transcriptionists to join their positions. Their normal pay for every minute of audio turns out to be around $0.6 for their standard jobs, yet they offer several forte assignments with higher pay rates.

- Payment methods: Direct deposits.

- Potential earnings: Transcriptionists are paid $0.60, on average, per minute of audio, in spite of the fact that there are several projects accessible on a regular basis that pay higher base rates because of their trouble.

- Available measure of work: Indeterminate, assignments are sent specifically to you by means of email. You are required to process no less than 4 hours of audio for every week.

- Joining requirements: Being a US citizen and breezing through a test, which includes translating a real audio clip.

- Link: http://www.fftranscription.com/join-team.html

3. Rev

Rev is entirely like the writing sites we secured in our writing segment, as in that you are free to pick your own particular work from an assignment pool. Every assignment has a different due date and rates that shift depending on a few elements, for example, accents, number of speakers, and urgency of the transcription.

- Payment methods: PayPal

- Potential earnings: Transcriptionists are paid $0.4-0.65 on average, per minute of audio. Rates change depending on the complexity of every assignment and are indicated at work pool before you accept any job.

- Available measure of work: There are always transcriptions accessible.

- Joining requirements: Passing a transcription test and having a PayPal account in order to get payments.

- Link: http://www.rev.com/freelancers/transcription

What Is A Penny Stock?

These stocks generally allude to any stock exchanging outside one of the leading major exchanges, like the NYSE, NASDAQ, or AMEX. These are frequently thought to be critical.

The meaning of a Penny Stock is a low-priced, speculative security, of a small organization, regardless of the business sector capitalization or whether it exchanges on a securitized trade like the NYSE or NASDAQ or an "over the counter" listing service, such as OTCBB or Pink Sheets. The terms Penny Stock, microcap stocks, small caps, and nano caps are new and are utilized conversely. However, the stock status is controlled by offer cost, not advertised capitalization or the listing service.

A Penny Stock, fundamentally, has business sector tops under $500M and are considered, to a great degree, theoretical, to those that exchange on low volumes over the counter. The Securities and

Exchange Commission cautions that these stocks can exchange, which implies that it can be hard to sell Penny Stock shares once you claim them.

It can be hard to acknowledge citations for a beyond any doubt Penny Stock, since they can be difficult to be precisely estimated. Investors would be prepared for the likelihood that they can lose their entire investment.

Can You Short Sell Penny Stocks?

As opposed to what a few traders trust, you are permitted to short sell penny stocks. This tends to astound/confound individuals, principally on the grounds that investopedia.com has stated in the past it was illegal, clearly this has been demonstrated off base by Tim Sykes. Learning to short sell makes you a more diverse and adaptable trader on the grounds that you can buy breakouts and short sell when the value drops. This gives you a unique ability to make profits in transit up and in transit down. Statistically, the chances ought to be to support you since each penny stock pump and dump will definitely fall 90% after the promotion. The crucial step is discovering shares to short before the stock crumbles.

When shorting small cap stocks, there are various factors that you ought to focus upon:

1. Allocating Shares to Short is Becoming Increasingly Difficult

Attempting to find shares to short can be truly troublesome and tedious. The margin rate is high when you attempt to hold these stocks in the long haul. Shorting will oblige you to open various brokerage accounts with a specific end goal to locate the best borrows. There is no single broker that will permit you to short sell each penny stock. In the event that you set up accounts with the top 4 brokers, this will permit you to short approximately 80% of your penny stock plays. In any case, every broker has diverse account minimums, therefore, short selling is not suitable for individuals with small account sizes. Some of the best brokers for short selling penny stocks are Interactive Brokers, Speedtrader, TradeStation and Suretrader. Brokers do not like the idea of short selling micro caps on the grounds that it is extremely dangerous because of potential short squeezes.

Suretrader

SureTrader is a Leading Online Broker for trading Stocks and Options

- Begin Trading with just $500

- No Pattern Day Trading Restrictions

- $4.95 Per-Trade + 6:1 Leverage

- Biggest Short-List with more than 10,000 symbols

- No Pattern Day Trading Rules

- Free $100k Trading Account Demo

Who can exchange with SureTrader?

- Persons outside the U.S.

- Trusts outside the U.S.

- Companies outside the U.S., for example, a U.K. company.

2. A Margin Trading Account is Needed

Keeping in mind that the end goal is to short sell, you need to exchange with margin, which is not required when buying penny stocks. Regardless, when exchanging with

J.A. Florentino

margin, you are acquiring cash from your stock broker. Many traders do not feel good borrowing from their broker. Additionally, more capital is required to open a margin account than a cash account in the event that you are required to set up half of the total position size that you need to short sell as collateral. This is known as initial margin. If the stock you short expands, then your margin levels will fall. At the point when your margin levels fall beneath 30%, your broker will have no real option except to issue a margin call. This compels you to deposit more cash into your account until your margin level is brought up to 50%. If you do not do this your position may be liquidated immediately. Penny stocks can spike 50-100% in a short space of time because of unanticipated circumstances, like a promoter conveying email alarms at random times throughout the day. You wind up losing cash purely because your timing was off.

3. Short Squeezes

When you short shares you are borrowing shares from somebody who has a position in the organization. The original owner of the penny stock may request their shares back at any time they want. This can bring about what is known as a "buy in", and can usually happen following a couple of days. A broker may issue a "buy in" if you are in a losing position on one of your short sells. You basically have little or no control of what happens, making you lose on the trade as the broker will buy back the shares at current market price. "Buy ins" cause short squeezes to increase the share price artificially as traders are being compelled to cover their shares at around the same value levels.

Let's look at the profile of the self-made millionaire trader who profits from and teaches the ins and outs of penny stocks. Even his students have now made over $16 million!

Timothy's Blog

Why He Started Blogging:

After bringing about great misfortunes in his past businesses, Timothy Sykes chose to compose a book enumerating his adventure

into dealing with the hedge fund and the lessons he learned from losing so much cash. Capitalizing on the web's capability, he then began a blog, with the objective of documenting the regulated procedure of transforming another $12,000 into millions.

Where He Is Now:

Tim is currently an author for AOL Finance and has been included on ABC, CNN, CBS, CNBC, FOX News, FOX Business Network, Reuters, and Business Week, to give a few examples. He was also featured in the TV show "Wall Street Warriors", on MOJO. His month to month blog income is in six figures and this is certainly one young fellow who ought to be checked out and learnt from.

www.TimothySykes.com

Conclusion

I tell individuals this more than once, and I will say it in this guide as well, your prosperity is 90% frame of mind and 10% execution. You can utilize the tips and traps laid out in this guide, however, without the

right mindset, you will not make any sort of progress.

What isolates successors from unsuccessful individuals is not their ability set as much as it is their mindset. There are individuals with no formal education that make more than those with PhDs. This may sound like hocus pocus, yet, it is most certainly not. Your mood influences all that you do in your life – the way you walk, talk, gesture, and generally introduce yourself. That comes through in the words you write, the work you do, and how individuals perceive you in each circumstance. Without a winning frame of mind, it does not make a difference what you do; you will not be fruitful in it.

I assume that you will get this going and you should trust that you have the ability and the mindset to get it going.